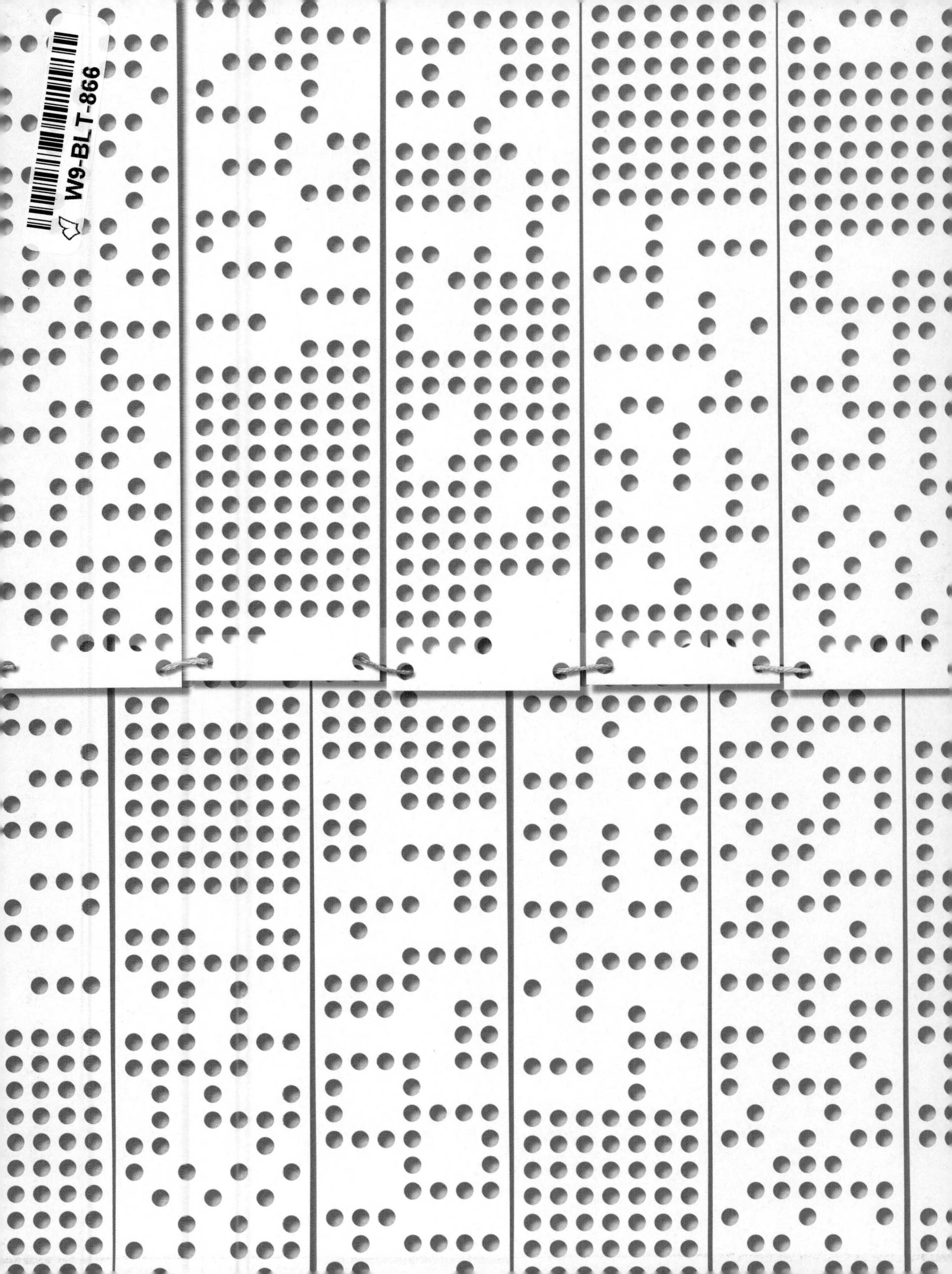

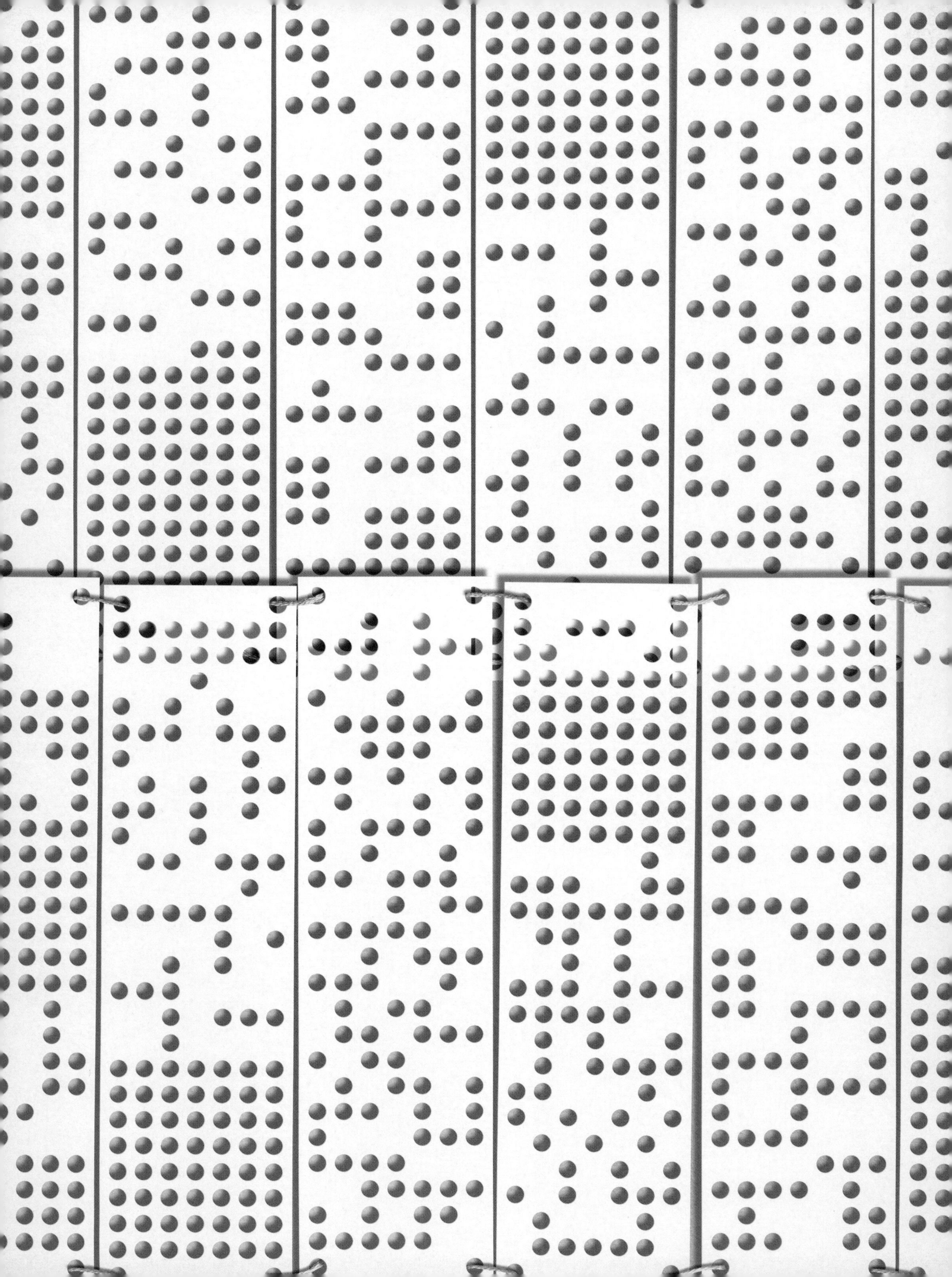

Fiona Robinson

The Story of *Ada Lovelace*, the
World's First Computer Programmer

Abrams Books for Young Readers
New York

Once there was a girl named Ada who dreamed of making a steam-powered flying horse.

Her mother despaired. She wanted Ada's feet planted firmly on the ground. She wanted her daughter to marry and lead the ordinary life of a nineteenth-century English lady.

But Ada Lovelace's ideas would carry her far above the ordinary. She would become the world's first computer programmer!

How was this possible, that a girl of her era could defy her strict mother and become a computer programmer before computers even existed? The story begins with her parents.

Ada's father was Lord Byron, a poet famous for his bold, imaginative writing. He was equally famous for his reckless ways. He spent money he didn't have and broke promises, even with those closest to him.

Ada's mother was Anne Isabella Milbanke, a wealthy woman, proper and ladylike. She was also a skilled mathematician who lived in a careful world of manners and numbers. Her husband called her the Princess of Parallelograms.

Poetry and parallelograms! Ada was born to parents who were very talented and very different. A month after Ada's birth on December 10, 1815, her mother, worried over her husband's wild ways, left him. She took baby Ada with her.

Ada never saw her father again. Her mother so feared that she would grow up to be imaginative and reckless like him that she covered his portrait with a cloth—as if he could influence Ada with his far-off, dreamy gaze.

Ada's mother thought her own favorite subject—mathematics—would keep her daughter steady and serious, so from a very early age Ada was encouraged to study numbers. Poetry was not allowed.

Little Ada had lessons of all kinds to keep her out of trouble. Here was her typical day as an eight-year-old:

10:00 A.M. Music

11:15 A.M. French Reading

11:30 A.M. Arithmetic

PRIMER OF FRENCH PROSE

Les Verbes

Le Dictionnaire

A French Primer

Le Français

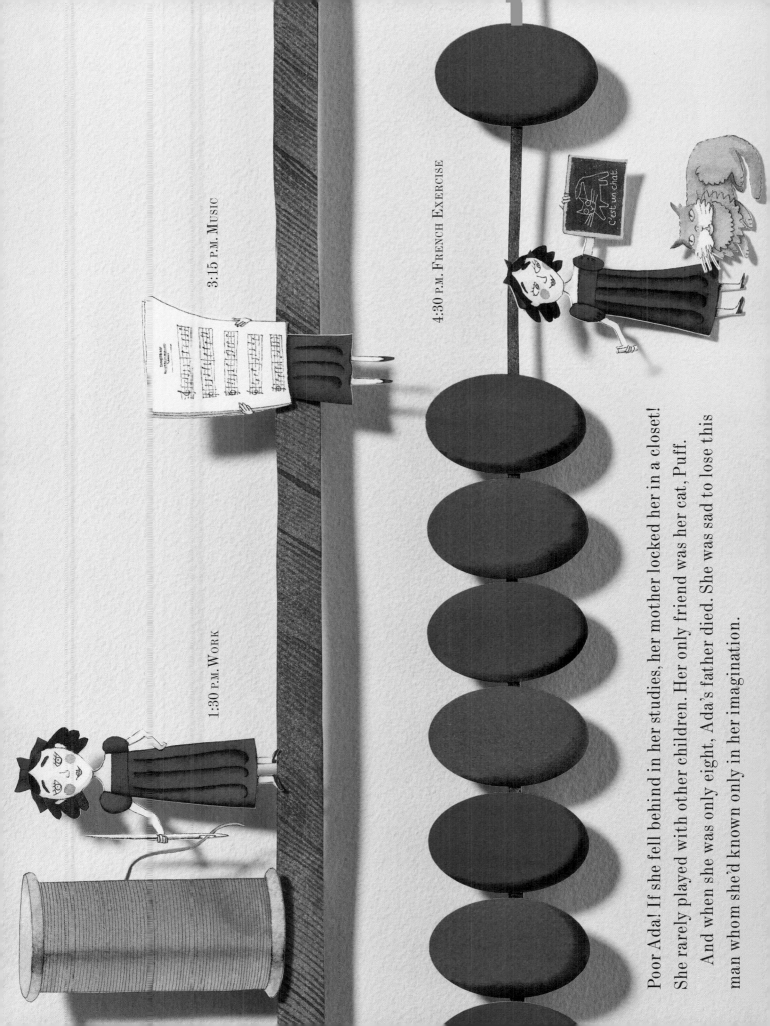

1:30 P.M. WORK

3:15 P.M. MUSIC

4:30 P.M. FRENCH EXERCISE

C'est un chat.

Poor Ada! If she fell behind in her studies, her mother locked her in a closet!
She rarely played with other children. Her only friend was her cat, Puff.
And when she was only eight, Ada's father died. She was sad to lose this
man whom she'd known only in her imagination.

Great changes were happening in the larger world, too. It was the Industrial Revolution! Factories and cotton mills appeared everywhere across the English countryside.

These buildings were filled with giant machines that whirred, clanked, and hissed with newly harnessed steam power. Engineers had used math and science to invent these machines, which made goods like cloth, glass, paper, and cement far more quickly than if they had been made by hand.

Touring the factories became a popular day out for the wealthy. The machines were thrilling modern wonders. Ada was fascinated by them. Her mother took her on trips to view these exciting new feats of engineering.

Her imagination whirred along with the powerful engines! And her mind, so well trained by her many lessons, began to invent!

She called one of her ideas . . .

… Flyology!

She wanted to invent a flying mechanical horse. Ada studied the wings of a dead crow and figured out how its feathers were ordered and attached. She wrote excitedly to her mother, who was traveling in Europe, of her flying plans, and she called herself "Your Affectionate Carrier Pigeon." Ada's mother despaired. Her daughter was beginning to remind her of Lord Byron. She sensed her imagination could not be confined by math, because Ada was starting to find her own sort of poetical expression … through math!

Before Ada's mother could ground her with more lessons, Ada was brought back to earth with a bump ... many bumps.

Ada fell ill with measles. She was so weak that for three years she could barely walk.

She put aside her dreams of flight and focused instead on her studies.

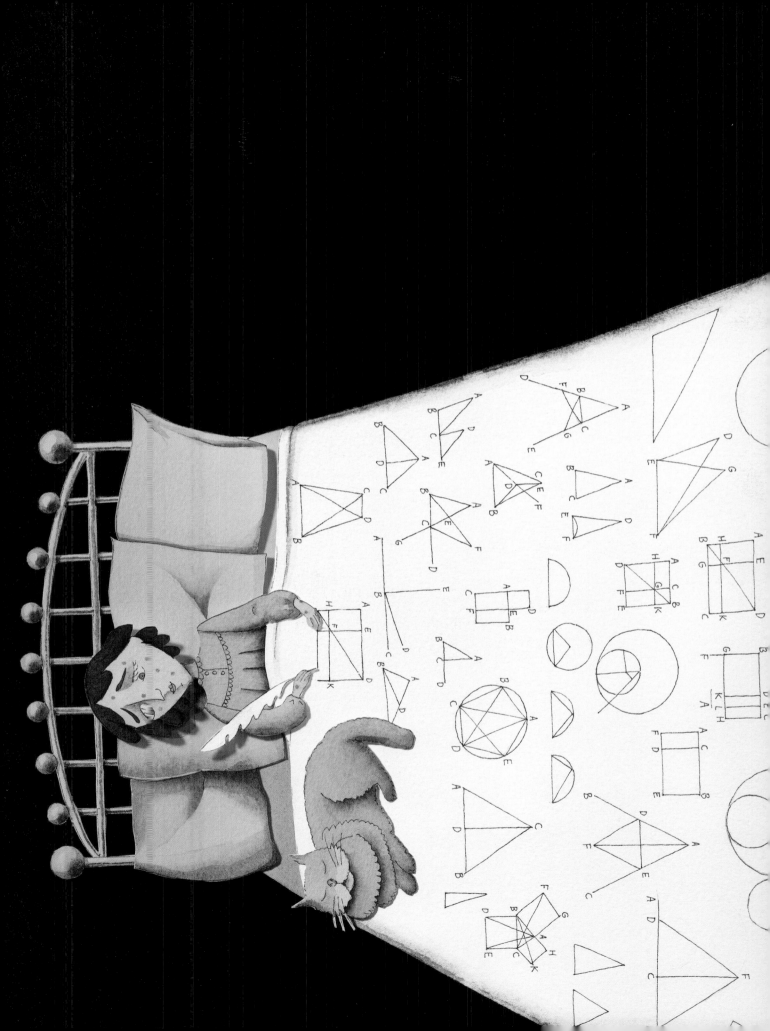

Happily, when she was sixteen, she recovered. Sixteen was an important age for a rich girl like Ada. It was when she was presented to the world as being eligible for marriage.

After her lonely childhood, Ada was suddenly thrust into society. Her mother encouraged her to dress in beautiful gowns and go to grand events like balls. Ada was thrilled to escape her quiet, regimented life and sickbed. Meeting writers, artists, politicians, and inventors re-ignited her imagination.

ADA'S MOTHER
always present,
keeping an eye on Ada

CHARLES DICKENS
famous writer

When she was seventeen, Ada met someone who would be very important to her future.
Not a potential husband, but an inventor named Charles Babbage.

MICHAEL FARADAY
scientist famous for his
experiments with electricity

MARY FAIRFAX SOMERVILLE
math genius and Ada's teacher and friend

CHARLES BABBAGE
engineer, mathematician,
and inventor

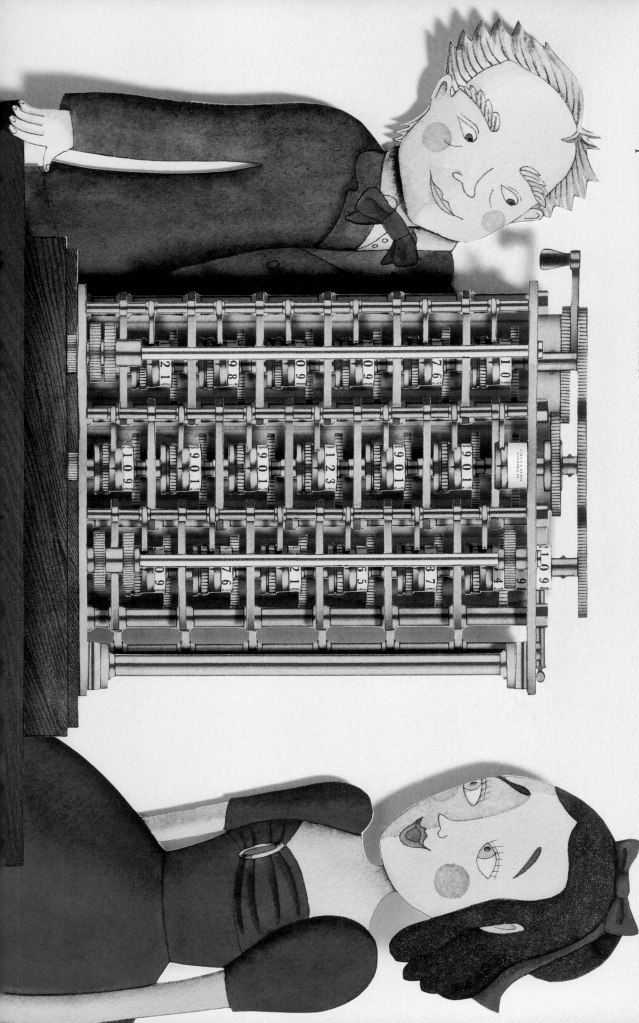

Mr. Babbage showed Ada part of his latest invention, *The Difference Engine.* When finished, it would be an enormous steam-powered calculator—heavier than an elephant and taller than a horse!

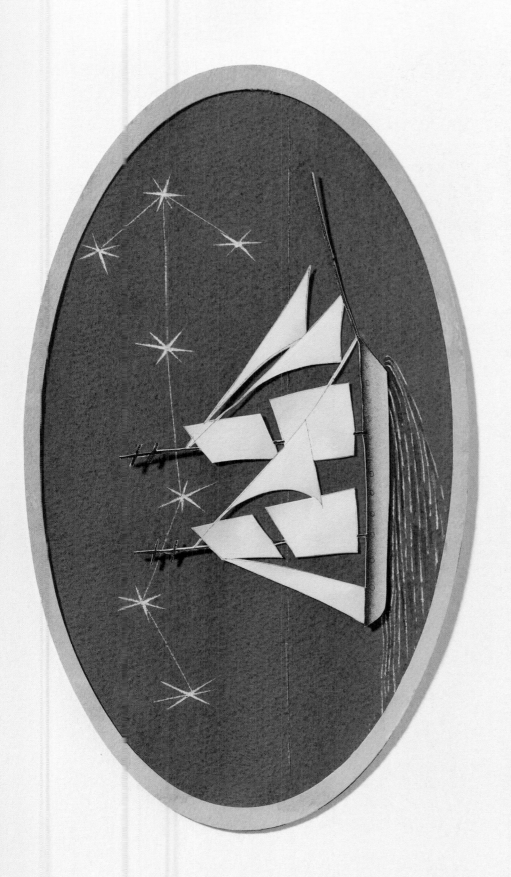

Mr. Babbage understood that human beings could make mistakes in math, and he was determined to create a machine that would always produce the correct answer.

His invention would be useful in many ways! One would be to help the ships that carried goods to and from England's factories. To orient the ships at night, when there was little to guide their course, navigators did calculations to measure the distance between stars. Mistakes in their calculations could cause ships to go off course. Mr. Babbage's machine would save time *and* lives!

Ada was thrilled by the Difference Engine! She became good friends with Mr. Babbage.

Her life changed in other ways, too. She married Lord William King, Earl of Lovelace, and had three children.

Despite her busy new life running a household of her own, Ada continued corresponding and meeting with Mr. Babbage to discuss his wonderful machines.

Mr. Babbage told her about his new invention,

The Analytical Engine.

This machine was designed
to be even bigger and better than
the Difference Engine. It would
perform many, many more calculations,
and store and print the results. Today,
it is generally agreed that this was
the world's first computer design.
Mr. Babbage explained to Ada that
the machine would be fed a series of
cards with holes that "told" it what to
do, an idea he had borrowed from
another machine.

Invented in 1801 by Joseph-Marie Jacquard, *The Jacquard Loom* made it possible to weave silk cloth with complicated and beautiful patterns. A string of punched cards was fed through the machine, and each card had a set of holes that corresponded to one line of the pattern. The machine would "read" these holes and then lift different threads in the cloth being woven, thereby creating the pattern.

Mr. Babbage intended for the Analytical Engine to work in a similar way. Each hole-punched card that was fed into his machine would tell it how to move to calculate sums. Ada excitedly offered to figure out the algorithm, or instructions, that would be punched into the cards. The punched cards were the machine's "program."

The algorithm Ada created was intended to program the machine to compute a complicated series of numbers called "Bernoulli numbers." Working out the algorithm for the program was a little like creating a treasure hunt inside a maze. Imagine that Ada was instructing you to find the treasures in a specific order. The treasures were the numbers she wanted the computer to calculate. She just had to give the machine the right directions, so it would find each number in turn.

$$B_8 = -\frac{1}{30}$$

$$B_{10} = \frac{5}{66}$$

$$B_6 = \frac{1}{42}$$

$$B_{12} = -\frac{691}{2730}$$

$$B_4 = -\frac{1}{30}$$

Ada says this is the start of the treasure
hunt and to take the green path!
There's the first number!

Ada says take the pink path!
Here's the second number!

Ada says follow the brown path!
Here's the third!

Now the purple path!
Fourth!

Now blue! Just around here
should be the fifth number!
You're on a roll! Here's the fifth!

Now orange . . .
. . . to the sixth! Ta-da!

And black to the seventh!

And yellow to the eighth.

Ada says you can leave this
maze or loop around on the white
path to find the numbers again!

$$B_{16} = -\frac{3617}{510}$$

$$B_2 = \frac{1}{6}$$

$$B_{14} = \frac{7}{6}$$

Ada also wrote about the potential of the Analytical Engine. Unlike Mr. Babbage, who thought it would just make calculations, Ada foresaw that a computer like the Analytical Engine would not be limited to math. She believed it could be programmed to create

pictures,

music,

and

words.

Anything that can be expressed as a sequence. This was a fantastic idea, but this is exactly what computers are capable of today!

Unfortunately, the Analytical Engine was never made. It would have cost too much money to build. Few people understood the impact it might have had. And, very sadly, Ada died young, at the age of thirty-six.

It took another one hundred years after Ada's death for the first working computers to be created in the United States and England.

The people who created them were stunned by Ada's futuristic notes and algorithm for Mr. Babbage's machine. Now Ada is widely considered the world's first computer programmer. For the girl who dreamed of steam-powered flying horses, a great imagination proved just as important as mathematical skill. With it, she saw a future no one else could envision.

A Note About Bernoulli Numbers

Bernoulli numbers are named after Swiss mathematician Jacob Bernoulli (1655–1705). They are a sequence of rational numbers—real numbers that can be expressed as fractions—and are very complicated to calculate. Ada said they were chosen as a "beautiful example" of how the Analytical Engine could be programmed to compute complex problems. Even Ada struggled with the algorithm, but she and Babbage aimed high! They wanted to show the extraordinary power of the Analytical Engine to do more than simple addition and subtraction.

• • •

Library of Congress Cataloging-in-Publication Data

Names: Robinson, Fiona, author.

Title: Ada's ideas : the story of Ada Lovelace, the world's first computer programmer / Fiona Robinson.

Description: New York : Abrams Books for Young Readers, 2016.

Identifiers: LCCN 2016004363 (print) | LCCN 2016009509 (eBook) | ISBN 9781419718724 (hardcover) | ISBN 9781613129135 (eBook)

Subjects: LCSH: Lovelace, Ada King, Countess of, 1815–1852—Juvenile literature. | Women mathematicians—Great Britain—Biography—Juvenile literature. | Mathematicians—Great Britain—Biography—Juvenile literature. | Women computer programmers—Great Britain—Biography—Juvenile literature. | Computers—Great Britain—History—19th century—Juvenile literature. | Computer algorithms—History—19th century—Juvenile literature.

Classification: LCC QA29.L72 R63 2016 (print) | LCC QA29.L72 (eBook) | DDC 510.92—dc23

LC record available at http://lccn.loc.gov/2016004363

Text and illustrations copyright © 2016 Fiona Robinson

Book design by Alyssa Nassner

Printed and bound in U.S.A.

10 9 8 7 6 5 4 3 2 1

Abrams Books for Young Readers are available at special discounts when purchased in quantity for premiums and promotions as well as fundraising or educational use. Special editions can also be created to specification. For details, contact specialsales@abramsbooks.com or the address below.

ABRAMS The Art of Books
115 West 18th Street, New York, NY 10011
abramsbooks.com

For S. V. M.

Artist's Note

• • •

The illustrations were created with Japanese watercolors on Arches paper. The paintings were then cut out using more than five hundred X-ACTO blades, assembled, and glued to different depths to achieve a 3-D final artwork. The images were then photographed.

• • •

Acknowledgments

I'd especially like to thank Jay Zukerkorn, who photographed and Photoshopped the final art. Thanks, too, to my editor, Susan Van Metre, and my designer, Alyssa Nassner. The Silk Museum in Macclesfield (UK), the Science Museum (London, UK), and the Museum of Science and Industry (Manchester, UK) were also a tremendous help. Thank you!

• • •

Bibliography

Essinger, James. *A Female Genius: How Ada Lovelace, Lord Byron's Daughter, Started the Computer Age.* London: Gibson Square Books, Ltd., 2013.

Moore, Doris Langley. *Ada, Countess of Lovelace: Byron's Legitimate Daughter.* New York: Harper and Row, 1977.

Stein, Dorothy. *Ada: A Life and a Legacy.* Cambridge: The MIT Press, 2004.

Toole, Betty Alexandra. *Ada, the Enchantress of Numbers: Prophet of the Computer Age.* Mill Valley, California: Strawberry Press, 1998.

Woolley, Benjamin. *The Bride of Science: Romance, Reason, and Byron's Daughter.* New York: McGraw-Hill, 2000.

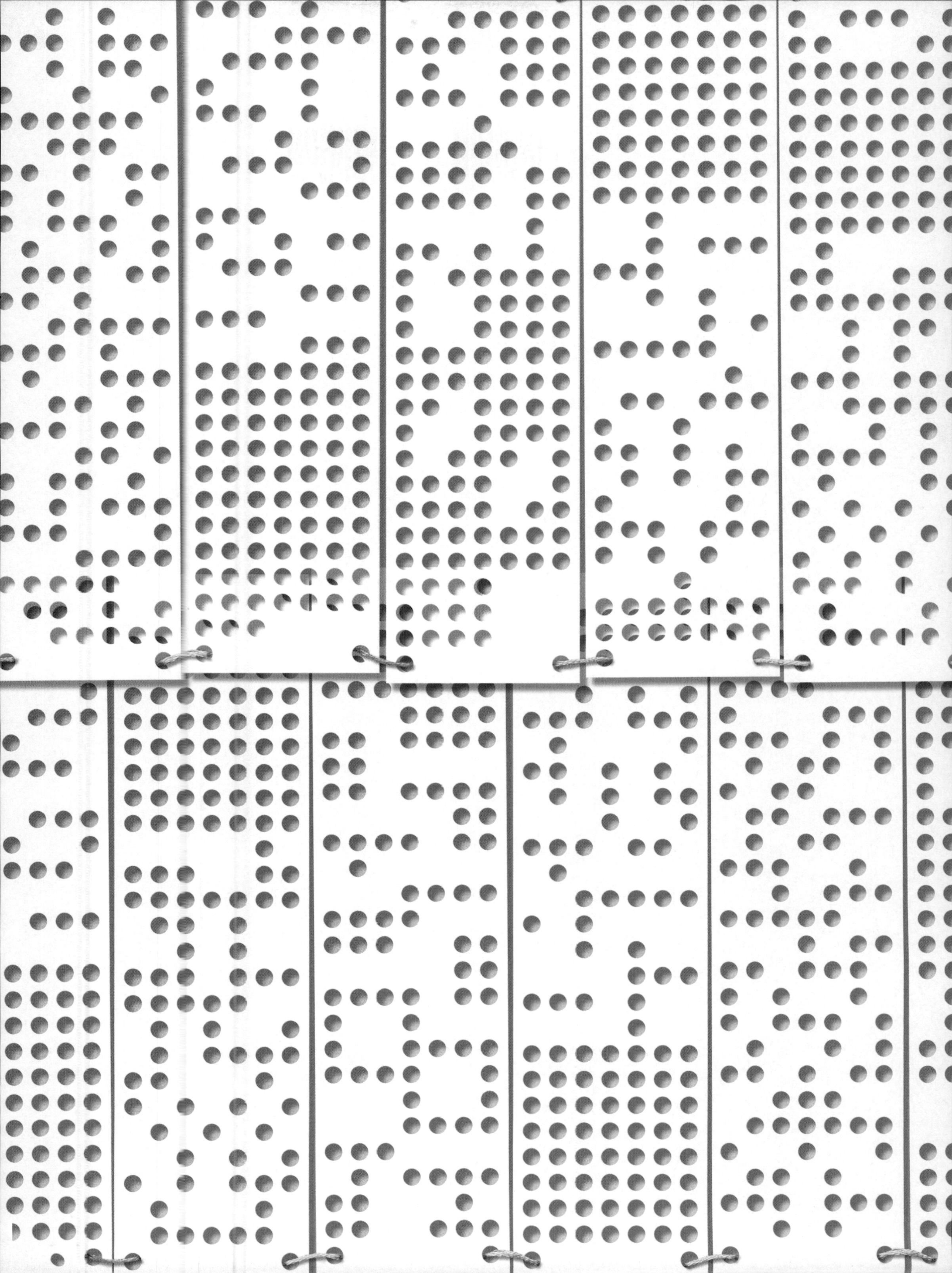

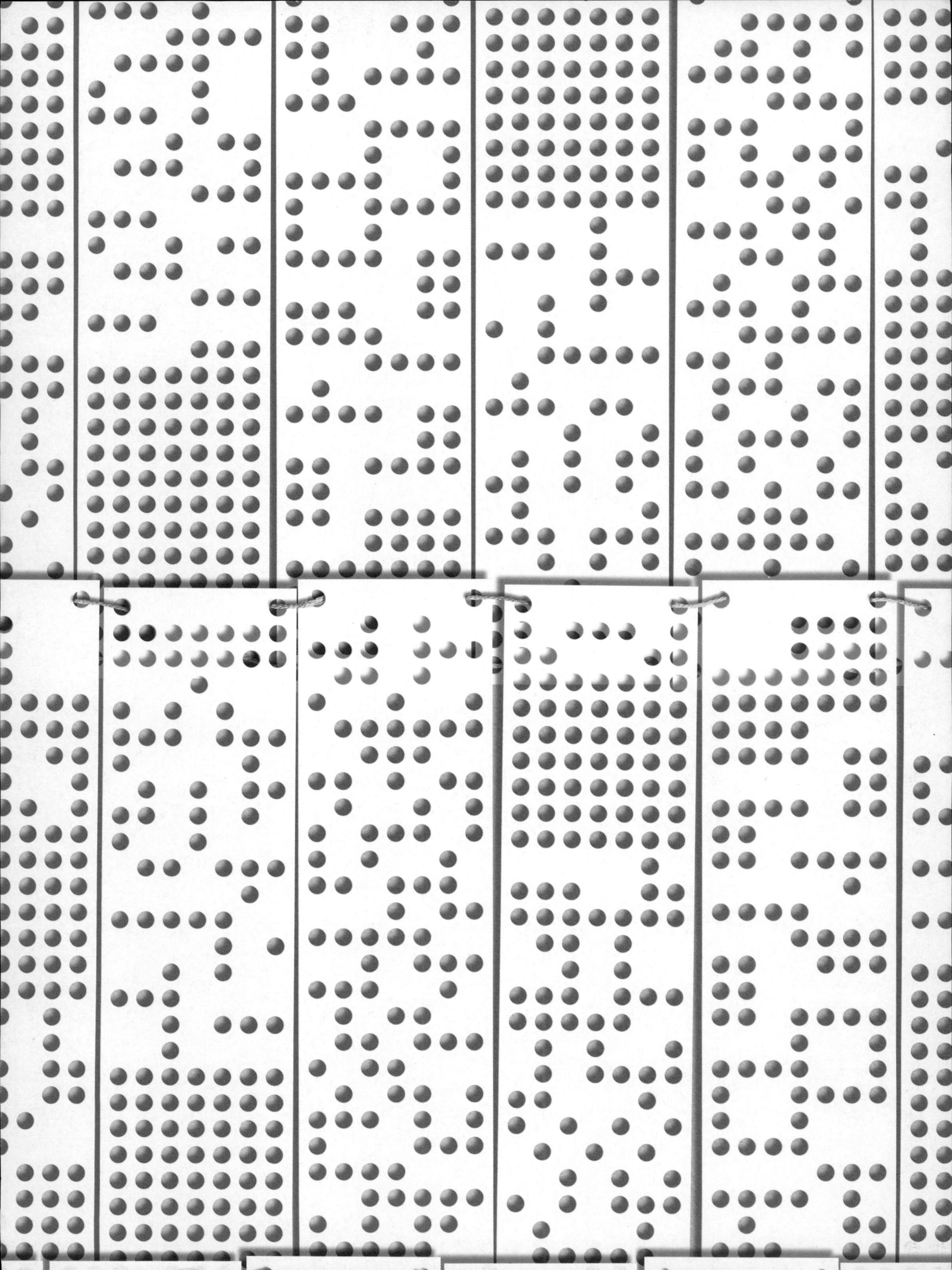